MW01492343

Sharing What I Know

Gail Alexander

PEN & PUBLISH

Saint Louis, Missouri

Published by

St. Louis, Missouri
(314) 827-6567
info@PenandPublish.com
www.PenandPublish.com

Print ISBN: 978-1-956897-49-4
e-book ISBN: 978-1-956897-50-0

This book is printed on the USA on acid-free paper.

Dedication:

To my fellow human beings who have challenged me, loved me, helped me during difficult times, laughed with me, uplifted me, and, most importantly, gave me a space to be fully myself.

Thank you!

Foreword

Many believe that a world teacher will appear when the time comes to transmute the game of earth we are playing to a more loving vibration. In this beautiful book, Gail and her guides teach you how to open and trust the process of sharing your unique vibration of the world teacher. By lovingly teaching you to "remember there is no right way, only your way" through her heartfelt and hilarious laugh-out-loud stories and channeled messages, we learn to surrender to, trust, and embody the flow of the wisdom and love that is our unity consciousness.

Thank you, Gail, for creating a book that graces humanity with the vibration of sharing the light of our soul by encouraging us to discover the "gifts and potential we are not even aware of." Gail is one of the most amazing souls I have met in this lifetime, and she has helped me embody the vibration of "I am blessed so that I can be a blessing."

—Julie A. Foster, MD, DABFM Medical Intuitive and Energy Healer

Table of Contents

Introduction

One night I was at dinner with friends talking about the books I had written. *I don't know how I know. . . I just know, and I still know what I know.* I always knew there would be a book three in this series as I usually do things in ones, threes, or fives. That night at 1 am, a working title popped in. What do I do with what I know? There isn't a truer question for me as I have been struggling with this since I wrote the first two books. The lingering question is, what do I do with the information I know? The Answer I heard was: TEACH. I heard that so loud and clear it surprised me. It was such a booming voice. Metatron, one of my main guides, just laughed and said, "It is about time."

I know my purpose is to help humanity ascend and for people to be the most authentic versions of themselves they can be. We are all lighthouses. It is up to each one of us to decide how brightly we want our light to shine, and to be a beacon to guide each other on our paths and home.

We are here on Earth to learn, grow, remember, love, and experience joy. Hopefully, this book brings a little light, a little laughter, a little joy, and a little wisdom to the world.

My spirit team is hilarious and often gives me information in jingles and song lyrics. When I am struggling and not connected, they (my spirit team) sing *the plug it in, plug it in* jingle to remind me that I need to connect.

One of their favorite songs, which they sing on repeat, is "Pure Imagination" from the original *Willy Wonka* movie. When we create our reality, we must be more intentional about what we create. My spirit team also sings, "This little light of mine; I'm going to let it shine," from time to time to remind me how important it is to let our light shine.

We all get signs, messages, and hunches all the time. The question is, are you paying attention? How often do you have to be smacked on the head with the proverbial 2x4 until you are willing to pay attention? Spirit can only do so much. The rest is up to us as to what we learn.

One of the things I have been sharing with people is that I do not like to be thoroughly grounded in the Earth because then I start to feel everything that will happen. So, my spirit team told me to picture myself wearing red magnetic clown shoes. Funny, I know, but they work. I bet that gave you a laugh when you thought about it. Every time I put on my red clown shoes and start walking around, I start laughing.

Over the last few years, I have become known as the no-nonsense intuitive because that is how I like to present information. Here it is with absolutely no sugarcoating. I tell you exactly what I am seeing, feeling, or hearing without filtering. The information comes through so fast that I don't have time to filter it.

I used to get so caught up in the idea that I was not doing it like everyone else; but no matter how much I tried to slow it down, I just couldn't. At some point, I finally realized and accepted how I work and get information. I did not need to be like anyone else. I just needed to be me, and that was enough. There will always be someone who does it differently or that you think is better than you because comparison is part of the human experience. However, that is just an illusion because we are all sparks of the divine, and there is no such thing as separateness. The more of us that wake up and realize we are all one, the more helpful it is to humanity and consciousness as a whole.

So, sit back and take a deep breath because, just like in the first two books, some things may challenge your beliefs and understanding of what is possible. Here we go: buckle up, keep your arms and legs in the vehicle at all times, and return your tray table to the upright and locked position. Spirit made me write that. They are just cracking up, and I hope you are as well.

I have much to cover, so let's dive in, shall we? I look forward to taking this journey with you.

Section One: The Unexplained and Unexpected Experiences

Being a Care Giver (Boundaries, Boundaries, Boundaries)

I have always had the kind of energy that made people want to talk to me about things. Even as a little kid, I understood relationships and people's energy. I remember people telling me I was going to be a therapist when I grew up, and I laughed at them and said no.

Well, that said, I did end up becoming a therapist. You might say the older I got, the more I grew into myself. I was a practicing therapist for 30 years, and I can tell you that being a caregiver can take its toll physically, psychologically, energetically, and spiritually. It is not about just sitting there and listening, which some therapists do. I would see everything on all levels. If clients were talking about their trauma, I would see and feel that as well. It took many years of practicing as a therapist to learn to set healthy boundaries around myself to keep from becoming depleted.

There are different degrees of care. The more significant toll for me was when a loved one was sick, and I was caring for them. It is imperative to know what you need for self-care and how to take good care of yourself. When traveling on airplanes, there is a reason why they tell you to put on your oxygen mask first before assisting others. If you pass out, you will not be of any help to anyone else. The same goes for caregiving. If you continue to give and give and give without reserving anything for your own well-being, you will get sick, have some crisis of your own, or be energetically depleted.

So, what does it mean to have healthy boundaries and take care of yourself? Different people will need different things as we are all wired differently. We are each a unique snowflake with no blanket recommendations other than sleep, food, and water. LOL.

I start with some downtime to decompress. As a practicing therapist, I always had about a 45-minute commute, which was helpful. I allowed myself to think about work and de-stress for the first half of the trip. When I reached the midway point in the commute it was time to switch gears and think about myself and what I needed to do in my life. Trust me, I know it is a lot harder than it sounds. Some nights I was so exhausted all I could do was veg out in front of the TV. The biggest things about being a caregiver are balance and setting and keeping healthy boundaries.

Being a caregiver is not about surrendering or sacrificing who you are to help others. Being of service as a caregiver is about balancing what you keep for yourself and what you have left to give away. If you receive 100 energy credits every day and they cannot roll over, how would you use them? Do you give all your energy credits away? Do you keep some for yourself? The answer will vary depending on what you are working through.

We are all guides for each other, walking each other on our paths and eventually home. We are not here to rescue anyone or fix things for anyone else. Everyone has free will, and what they do is up to them. Being kind pays a more significant dividend without costing more.

Questions to ask yourself:

How much of my energy am I giving away?

What is my practice for self-care?

How do I nurture myself?

Do I rest when I am exhausted, or do I keep pushing?

Choosing Health: My Experiences with Illness

I have had allergies for as long as I can remember. Somewhere along the line when I was in college, I had mono and was on a ton of antibiotics. I was prescribed penicillin, which I had used previously when needed, for my entire life with no problems.

My father took me to Las Vegas for my 21st birthday present a year after my birthday. While we were there, I was going from heat to air-conditioning and sweating. I didn't think about it at the time. On the plane home, the top of my head was itching; it was the 10th day on the antibiotic.

The next day I saw a doctor who told me to go home and shower, saying I must have rubbed up against something. Well, by two in the morning, I was covered in golf ball and softball size welts and having trouble swallowing. So, what did I do? If you said "Go to the ER," you would be incorrect. I took my Benadryl and drove to my parents' house while sucking on hard candy to keep me swallowing.

My mother took one look at me and made an emergency call to the allergist. The allergist told her to make a baking soda and water paste to cover the welts and instructed me to keep taking Benadryl. He would see me the next day. But, if it got any worse, we should go to the ER.

I saw the allergist the next day and got put on steroids to stop the reaction. However, everything hurt, and I got pretty sick. I had just started with a new doctor as I was now an adult and had graduated from grad school, so seeing my pediatrician wouldn't work. He ordered a bunch of blood tests, and that was how we discovered I had serum sickness. The penicillin had poisoned my entire body like a snake bite. I was lucky to be alive. Thank you, angels, spirit team, and helpers.

My doctors told me I needed to lay low, rest, and take it easy. Everything hurt, and I couldn't even sit up because the pain was so bad. The doctors told my parents that all of my internal organs were swollen and inflamed and could rupture at any point. I did not know what was happening or how bad it was, which was probably good.

This experience laid the foundation for some of the other experiences I had. After that happened, when I got sick and needed an antibiotic, no matter what antibiotic it was, within the first two doses I broke out in hives and welts. I had also developed allergies to many foods at this point and I had chronic migraines for two years until they figured out which foods were causing them.

Finding out what I can and cannot tolerate has been quite a dance. As I learned more about energy, metaphysics, and such, some of what happened corresponded to times I leveled up spiritually.

My first strange experience with surgeries was with my two orthoscopic knee surgeries. I was already familiar with some of my gifts by then, so while waiting in the pre-op room for the surgeon who was running late, I kept myself occupied by playing with my heart rate; slowing it down and speeding it up. While doing that, I had a conversation with my spirit team. I said, "I am here; I am going to have the surgery anyway. Can you just move it so that the surgery is less invasive and goes quickly?" I am not kidding when I say that my surgery was less than 15 minutes. Thank you, spirit team, angels, and helpers. After the surgeries, at my follow-up visits, the nurse said the doctor would come in, show me the pictures, and go over everything that happened. The doctor did not explain anything about either of my surgeries nor did he want to talk at all about them with me.

In another incident, I was in severe pain on my right side. I went to the ER and was told that I needed to have a CAT scan. When I got to radiology, they said I had to wait in the hallway. Something happened in the room that had never happened before. The dye they were going to use during the procedure exploded everywhere. When I finally got in for the test, I asked what ingredients were in the dye. They said iodine. I said I am deathly allergic to iodine. Again, thanks spirit team, angels, and helpers.

Next came the surgery to have my gallbladder removed. I got into many arguments with the anesthesiologist because I am allergic to all antibiotics. Needless to say, I had surgery without any antibiotics, you can only imagine the forms they made me sign. I also cannot have any pain meds or ibuprofen. So, after the surgery, they kept trying to give me ibuprofen and pain meds that I was allergic to. Since my surgery was late in the day, they wanted me to stay overnight. I told them that if I could go home, I would prefer that because they kept trying to make me take medications that I was allergic to. Again, trust yourself and your intuition. I knew something was going to happen that was not going to be good if I had stayed. I ended up being able to go home around 8 pm and luckily a friend of mine agreed to stay overnight with me at my apartment.

The next medical experience was after both of my parents transitioned. I had a mammogram on the anniversary of my mom's passing. I was off work and should have put two and two together that something was going to be up. Again, I am in a human body and I did not think about it. Needless to say, I had the mammogram on August 14th and got a call later that day that something showed up and I needed to go for more testing.

I freaked out, scheduled the diagnostic tests, and after the two tests, I was told I needed to meet with the radiologist. That is never a good sign. I was escorted into an office and told that I had stage zero breast cancer and I needed to have a biopsy and lumpectomy. In the meantime, I started talking to friends about it. I asked my friends to send me healing energy for my highest good and place me on prayer lists. It is important to cover all your bases. The spot targeted for the biopsy was underneath and hard to get to, so they physically torqued my body into the strangest positions in the freezing room for over four hours as they just couldn't reach the spot during the biopsy. I kept my attitude positive and talked to my body stating I did not need to have this experience just for the lesson, that I understood I needed to take better care of myself. I didn't realize how depleted I had become over the last five to seven years from taking care of and supporting both parents along with their medical issues at the ends of their lives.

The results were back, and I had my appointment with the surgeon. The surgeon was talking to me about options and if it was cancer, what that meant. Every medical professional I talked to kept telling me it was cancerous. I looked right at the surgeon and was surprised at what came out of my mouth. I said cancer does not work for me, and this is not going to be malignant. The surgeon just looked at me like I was nuts. Surgery was now scheduled in a few weeks. The whole process was less than two months, as they wanted to get it out before it got worse.

I had the surgery; the results came back and it was all negative. Being who I am, when I had my follow-up appointment with the surgeon I said, "See, I told you it was not going to be cancerous." My report said the findings were discordant because the results did not match what everyone was telling me.

Fast forward two years. More family members were sick and going through things. I was depleted again because I put all my effort into energetically helping and supporting my family members. It was time again for my annual mammogram. I had a clean one the previous year, then this one came back with a spot on the same side as the previous bad results, and back I went to get biopsies. This time it was an easier spot to reach and the results came back negative. No further action needed to be taken. I was extremely grateful and said thank you, angels, spirit team, and helpers.

Our attitude drives what happens in our energy field. How we take care of ourselves, or not, plays a role in our physical health. Everything is in our energy field and if we do not attend to the things that affect our energy, it manifests in our physical body to force us to care for ourselves and pay attention.

Next situation: I had to get all the COVID-19 vaccines for work, and starting at the second dose, I had some issues. I started stuttering and I had never done that before. I had five vaccines in two years. I had to get them at the recommended rate for healthcare professionals. During that time, I was having more and more allergic reactions to things, and after one trip to the ER for an allergic reaction I was given a name and an appointment with an allergist to follow up with. Since this was still during active covid times, most of my first appointments were virtual.

I kept telling the allergist that I was having hives every day and the treatment was to take 4x the amount of allergy medicine. I followed that advice, and the hives got worse. I asked the allergist to write me a note to not have any more vaccines because I was having constant reactions. She stated she was not able to do that. She told me that she had made patients who had anaphylactic reactions get the second dose. I was so sick and worn down with the chronic hives. Every interaction with that doctor was a test to see how much more invalidation she could shovel at me. This was also happening in the same time frame as the second round of biopsies. Since the allergist was not willing to work with me to figure it out and kept repeating over and over again it was nothing I was eating, I finally decided to get a second opinion. I had begun to re-tune into the fact that I know my own body and I know what an allergic reaction feels like.

My friend recommended this great allergist who had been practicing for over 30 years. I walked in and explained what happened to this compassionate, attentive new doctor. They tested me first for food allergies. It turns out everything I was currently eating was causing problems. I was also allergic to the binding agent found in all over-the-counter medications and vaccines that the first doctor was prescribing. All of those allergens together were causing months of dystonic reactions and chronic hives. Things immediately got better when I changed my diet and stopped the allergy meds that contained the binder I was allergic to. It's a good thing I got a second opinion and trusted my body and intuition. You know yourself better than anyone else.

The reason I am sharing these personal stories is we have all been through things. We have all received information we then measured against what we knew about our body. It is important to be heard and be able to trust the people you are working with, and when things don't feel right, it's important to seek other advice. The first allergist saw me as a problem and as a hypochondriac and told me I needed to just live with the hives instead of doing anything useful or helpful to try and figure out what was going on. That methodology just did not work for me knowing myself as well as I do and being who I am. So, once I had a doctor who listened and helped me with the food allergies, I got down to the business of paying attention when an allergic reaction happened. Then the hives started to get better.

Questions to ask yourself:

How have my thoughts impacted my health?

What are some tribal and familiar beliefs I have that are currently impacting my health?

What does it bring up for you when you think about being the master of your destiny and that the decisions you make affect your health?

Surgeries and the Unexplained

This section of the book talks about experiences I have had with loved ones, surgeries, and the unexplained things that happened during those procedures.

First, let me just say that my family was never open to talking about or discussing anything metaphysical. If you read book one, *I don't know how I know . . . I just know.* You know that I was silenced as a kid because of what I knew and how much it scared the adults around me. So, these experiences are remarkable when you start to think about how far my family has come.

The first experience I'll describe happened when my mother was diagnosed with Multiple Myeloma. She was in the hospital at the time and almost died from sepsis. I talked about that in an earlier book. My mother needed a port put in to receive chemotherapy, and she was scared about that procedure. Her oncologist, the doctor doing the procedure, and the nurses were all trying to comfort her to no avail. Then she refused to have it done. After about 30 minutes a new doctor walked in at the start of his shift and his energy calmed my mother down. She finally agreed to have the procedure.

At this point I was no longer scared of sharing things with people so I said, "Don't worry Mom, I will fill the operating room with angels and helpers. You will not be alone, and everything will go smoothly. You will be okay." She took a deep breath and seemed to relax. The procedure did not take long, and the nurse came out to tell me it was over. Then she said the oddest thing happened. The machines all went screwy. They all backed away for a few seconds and then the machines corrected themselves. No one touched anything, but they just all came back online, glitch fixed. All of them in the operating just looked at each other. The nurse said to me, "I remember what you said about sending helpers and angels." She said some force intervened and they had never seen that before, and it made a believer out of her after seeing it with her own eyes. The nurse then said thank you. I was just grateful my mom was okay and got through the procedure. I thanked all the angels and helpers who were with her during the procedure and for making everything go as smoothly as it could.

The second experience with a loved one was when my dad needed to have a surgical procedure and was nervous while we were sitting there waiting for him to be taken in. I believe it was his hip replacement surgery. So, I sketched a mandala of angels and made sure it could stay with him. I also said don't worry Dad, I will send angels and helpers and you won't be alone. That mandala sketch was in the O.R. and then followed him back to his hospital room. I then got a message so loud and clear that I needed to go home immediately to create a healing mandala and bring it back to the hospital before visiting hours were over. I knew to follow this guidance.

I brought the mandala back and my dad said thank you. The next morning, he starts telling us that his blood sugar dropped so low that he almost died. The staff had given him the incorrect dosage of insulin. He said it was the mandala that caused it and I said that if the mandala and that energy were not in your room, you would not be here now.

The third experience I'll share is that one of my loved ones was scheduled to have a surgical procedure. I was apprehensive because both of my grandfathers and my great-grandfather whom I had never met, all appeared to me the day before the surgery. I wondered what was going to happen.

The day of the procedure I did what I usually do and asked the operating room to be filled with angels, helpers, and doctors from the Casa in Brazil that work with me from time to time. On the day of the surgery, it turned out to be two surgeries as the first one did not go as planned. During that time, my loved one was floating in my apartment talking to me. I had a feeling my loved one was trying to decide if they were going to stay or leave. They were surrounded by white light, full of peace and love. My loved one was outside of their physical body and having conversations with many different people from the other side. I could see and talk to my loved one very easily. I assured them that whatever they wanted to do was okay and that I loved them very much and just wanted them to have peace. I let my loved one know that I would support them in whatever decision they needed to make and help with that decision.

At night I put my loved one in a DNA healing cocoon which is something I do for people to help their auric layers heal.

The next day I could still feel my loved one's indecision about staying. The gifts of being highly intuitive are complicated. I saw family members from the other side talking to my loved one. I could see it all happening as clear as day. My mother, who was on the other side, asked if I could see this. I said yes. She said this isn't something you are meant to see. I told my mother I could see it; I just did not know what was being said. My spirit team made some adjustments after that so I could no longer see the conversations and options being given.

The next couple of days my loved one came mostly in the mornings and talked to me. Due to circumstances, free will, and choices, talking on the physical human level was not always easy for us. I answered questions and just kept telling him that whatever choice he made was okay. My loved one felt safe knowing he was still connected here and could be seen.

One morning I was in tears and was told to write down what my loved one was saying to me. It was a goodbye. I was asked to give messages to other family members and he apologized and made peace. This was one of the options my loved one was given but ultimately it wasn't the one he decided to take.

Who do you talk to about experiences like this because they make you seem a little crazy? Again, coming from a mental health background, I have always been careful about whom I choose to share the things I see with.

Two things I know and have learned from this experience is that we never know how much time we are going to have with someone, and we cannot interfere with free will. I learned to send energy for the highest good and the highest good of all those involved.

My loved one was in ICU for 10 days or so. I could always tell when they gave them more pain meds and how much pain he was in as he would come talk to me and we would both be in white light – in the space between. I had never really thought about our bond or connection before and was surprised to see and feel how connected we were, as that had not played out in the physical world. Here we are every day having conversations, and I would just listen to whatever they wanted to talk about. It was surreal, to say the least.

The biggest thing I learned from this experience was he was out of his body often, and when out of the body in the space between this and the other side, there is no pain, only love and light.

My loved one asked if I would continue to send the light and love he was experiencing when he was back in his physical body. I said I would. My loved one liked the peace of the light and it helped with giving him a space to explore and see what direction he wanted to go. My loved one is still recovering and is different. My loved one has more peace within where there used to be anger. Light and love can heal.

Some days I feel him more and some days less. The struggles we had no longer seemed to matter or exist. There is just peace, love, and understanding. I understood why my loved one made some of the choices they did and how they have been able to transcend those experiences and now realize how important love, peace, and support are in life.

The individual who is experiencing surgery, illness, or transition is having their journey, and the people around them who are supporting them by praying or perhaps sending love and light, also have a journey. It is a shared experience and memory, but not the same for everyone involved. Each soul takes something different from each experience. Sometimes in the busy world we live in, we forget how connected we are.

Questions to ask yourself:

What kind of experiences have I had where I knew things that were going on but did not feel like I could say anything?

How many times when you had loved ones going through procedures you just knew, felt, or saw things you didn't think you should know, see or feel?

Experiences with Death, Dying, and the Unexpected

I talked about my mom's illness in *I Still Know What I Know,* therefore, I am not going to go into a lot of detail here. But as her illness progressed and she got closer to her transition, my mother was terrified of dying. So, I had a conversation about death and dying with her and answered any questions she had. So my times I had to call ambulances, and so many times she was so close to transitioning. I could feel all her fear. I cried each time I followed the ambulance to the hospital, and during the trip had conversations with my mother's guides, angels, and higher self and said whatever she needed to do was okay and that we would all be okay.

About three weeks before she transitioned, we had a conversation and she said it was strange, that she had a dream with a loved one who had transitioned. In the dream one of her aunts, whom she was close to, came in and my mom said it was so real, it was like she was there talking to me. In my head, I said that wasn't a dream it was a visitation, and I chose to listen while my mom shared her experience. Even though I knew what was happening, she needed to have the experience to make sense for her and her beliefs, so I did not say anything. Now that my mother was being visited by my loved ones who had transitioned, I knew there was not much time left.

When it was my mom's time, I was in the hospital room and I saw my aunt reach down to escort my mother home. My mother said I will not leave with my daughter here. I was told what time my aunt would be coming back, and I needed to leave. My mother thought she was sparing me from something, so I honored the request. I could also see and feel all the transport angels around her. As soon as I got home, I got a call from the hospital letting us know she transitioned. Even though I knew it was happening, and the timing of it, getting the phone call where it became real did not make it any easier to manage all the feelings.

Another example was when my good friend Jeannette, who I knew from metaphysical classes I took at the beginning of my journey, was dying of cancer. I struggled for days about whether I should go see her and what would happen if I did. After much back and forth I decided to go and see her and I took a rose quartz crystal with me. I cannot remember if it was Saturday or Sunday when I went.

I walked over to her and let her know I was there. I put the rose quartz crystal in her hand and all of a sudden she opened her eyes, put the crystal on her heart and said, "I have been waiting for you Master." Well, this freaked the H. E. double hockey sticks out of me. After my interaction with her, I was talking to her husband whom I knew, and her son whom I had just met that day. Her husband and son talked about her resistance to letting go; they just wanted her to be at peace. They both knew about some of my gifts and abilities and had watched the interaction I had just had with Jeannette. They both turned to me and asked me when I thought she would transition. I said Thursday, and told them in my meditations I would come get Jeannette for the next couple of days and we would go to the other side so there would be no fear.

I had previously done this with my grandmother who was also afraid to let go so I knew I would be able to do it. I do not like to promise people something I know is not possible to do. So, Thursday rolled around and I just sat waiting for the phone call as I could feel her letting go. Jeannette transitioned peacefully at 11:11 am Thursday with her family around her.

Luckily, I knew many other people going to the funeral because I knew energetically it was going to take a toll on me. All funerals take a toll on me no matter how well I know the person who transitioned, or as the Hawaiians say, changed addresses. Thinking about it that way brings me more of a sense of peace.

In the days leading up to the funeral I could see, talk to, and feel Jeannette close by, so that was not difficult for me. Halfway through the funeral, I saw her go fully into the light and could feel the love and peace and she said goodbye and thank you. Needless to say, all of a sudden in the middle of the funeral I started sobbing but really could not share what had happened.

I had a friend Veronica who was very much on the metaphysical path and we had so many different conversations over the years about so many different things. We also met in a healing class, a different class than the one I met Jeannette in. Veronica had struggled with her health ever since I knew her and needed to have her hip replaced. She was also dealing with several types of cancer. After the hip replacement, she was at a rehab facility near my house. On Sunday afternoon she started telepathically communicating with me because she liked to do that instead of using the phone. She always found it funny that I could hear her. Back to the story. So around 1 pm I heard her and felt her and it went on all afternoon. She said, "I need you to come there is something I need." At 5 p.m. I showed up at the rehab facility asking what she wanted and she just started laughing. I said next time, pick up the phone and call me like a normal human being which just made her laugh harder. Then Veronica said she didn't like what they were serving for dinner, so I need you to go out and get me something else. I said you summoned me for this and we were both laughing at this point. I went out and got what she wanted for dinner and brought it back for her.

A few years after this her health started deteriorating and she was on dialysis. It was not going to be much longer. Veronica and I were part of a group of five friends who all met in this class. We all gathered at the facility she was at. She was having dialysis at the time. Her body was swollen and I could feel death and peace at the same time. She opened her eyes and looked at me as if to say yes, I know, it is going to be okay. I was trying everything I could not to cry at the time, but of course, I broke down as soon as I left.

A few days later I woke up and knew she had transitioned. Right after that my phone rang and it was the facility. I was listed as the emergency contact and they could not get a hold of her son who was exhausted and had shut his phone off. I tried multiple times to call him and the facility tried to call and the facility kept calling me. Finally, we had to send the police to the house to wake him up and tell him.

When people are terminal, I can tell when they are going to transition. Knowing it does not make it any easier when you get the news.

A few months later, my good friend Peter was diagnosed with bladder cancer. Peter was an amazing human being and healer and just let his light shine to whoever needed it. He was one of the most compassionate, loving people I had ever met. He felt very Jesus-like energetically. Peter and I used to trade

energy sessions. I have to be honest, I questioned why this internationally admired and loved healer wanted to trade sessions and spend time with me, and yet he did.

The first time I met Peter was at his home. A group of us got together to talk about healing, energy, and metaphysics. I remember feeling an instant connection to him. Back to the story.

Peter came home from the hospital after the diagnosis and requested that I visit him. I had made him a crystal healing grid and brought some healing mandalas as well. I did not have a good feeling, but Peter promised me he was not going to leave. He was going to stay and fight. I was going away for the weekend to a friend's lake house. I was about an hour into my four-hour trip and I started crying while driving as I saw him leave and cross over. I was mad at first as he promised he wasn't going to go, but we both knew that wasn't true. Sure enough, a few minutes later my phone rang from a mutual friend and I said Peter transitioned. She asked how I knew and I said I saw it and felt it. We were very connected. In that last conversation I had with Peter he made me promise that if he transitioned, he wanted a mandala of his energy for his family. I honored the commitment and gave his family the mandala at the funeral.

Peter and I still have a very strong bond and I talked about it in one of my other books. One night when my mother was actively dying, Peter came in and sat with her so I could get some sleep. He knew I was exhausted.

The mother of one of my good friends I have known forever was transitioning. My friend asked me if I knew when it would be. I said are you sure you want to know? Sometimes that makes it more difficult. My friend said yes, she wanted to know. I told my friend the information I was given. I got a call from her after her mother transitioned or changed addresses and she said I was right. As I said earlier, we all still need to navigate the humanness of all our feelings and emotions. I shared my condolences with her and of course, in a few days her mother came through and I gave my friend the message.

I had another loved one who was in the process of transitioning and I was on a phone call with another friend of mine and all of a sudden, I threw my arms up in the air and said woohoo. My friend was like, what just happened? I said my uncle just transitioned and he was reunited with his biological family that he had lost in the war and holocaust. When he transitioned, I had a vision of him as a little boy running around outside, and he was just so happy and at peace being reunited with his family – it brought tears to my eyes. Sure enough, within five minutes my father called to tell me my uncle had just transitioned.

For a while, I gave myself the nickname Angel of Death because that is what it felt like. I have learned so much from these experiences and even more from all the people who have transitioned and changed addresses. There are too many of these stories to share here. I am sure many of you reading this have had similar experiences or experiences with death and dying. We must start to have conversations about it as it is a part of life. None of us are getting out of here alive.

Questions to ask yourself:

Have you had a premonition about something before it happened?

When someone is sick, have you just known when they transitioned?

What are your thoughts about death and dying?

How do those thoughts impact the decisions you are making in your life now?

Near, Near Death Experience

I did not think I would ever be talking about this, but apparently, I am. And I get to say that Spirit made me do it. LOL. So, here goes. Say what you will about this, and take away what you will, but it is important to include for some reason. I am past the point of asking why they keep putting certain thoughts in my head over and over until I sit down and type them out. So, keep an open mind as you read this and think about if you have ever had an experience like this.

I have thought about the following experience often in my life trying to understand it because I knew it was a turning point for me. When I was 17 years old, I was driving to high school one day and the roads were icy. Although I was in a 4-wheel drive vehicle at the time, it was no match for the black ice. A semi-truck was coming at me and there was nowhere for me to go. My heart was pounding and I was like I am not getting out of this alive. All of a sudden I felt this sense of peace and knew I was going to be okay and fully supported. Miraculously, the semi stopped ½ inch from my vehicle. Years later I remember reading one of the *Conversation with God* books by Neale Donald Walsch and he was talking about how sometimes you do die but it is not your time to go so you are put back in the situation and it has a different outcome. At least, that is what I took from the book.

All I remember from the fateful day with the semi-truck and the ice right before I would have had impact, was the overwhelming calm I felt. After it was over I drove to school like nothing happened. What did happen? I believe I was hit in the accident and crossed over to the other side, but it was not my time to go so I was brought back with the best possible outcome of no accident. There is no way that we could have both stopped on that black ice.

The point or reason that spirit wanted me to talk about this is because we have all had experiences like this whether we are conscious of them or not. When it is not your time, it is not your time. It is really that simple. Back to the part of near-death experiences. There is so much research and information out there now about it that more people are considering it a possibility. But, what about all the times we have near-death experiences where you can't prove that you crossed over for a split second but you know you did? Spirit wanted me to talk about and share this because many people have had experiences like this. Again, we need to get comfortable talking about all these things because they are happening. It is a possibility. We need to expand our awareness and how we think about and process things. There is so much more going on than we are aware of.

Questions to ask yourself:

Is there an experience like this that came up for you while you were reading this?

Do you know anyone where you have said how did you walk away from that?

How have these experiences changed you?

Section Two: Guidance

Angels, Arch Angels, Ascended Masters, Loved Ones and Multidimensional Beings

In this section, we are going to talk about figuring out who you are working with and what messages are coming through. One thing I want to say is that my guides are funny or at least that is how they come through to me, because being human is full of emotions and distress.

I have got to be honest with all of you that following without questioning or having doubts is not one of my strong suits. As I shared in book one, I was a very reluctant mystic and never saw myself where I am now. My, how the tide has turned. As I continued to follow the messages, they became clearer and easier to understand. I feel like I finally got the decoder ring. If I can get the decoder ring, so can you.

Ashtar, Metatron, and Jesus walk into a bar... I am just typing what I am hearing. They (my spirit team) are laughing because I usually never follow directions without questioning as I just shared. In all seriousness, these are the guides that I work with the most and are around me the most. They all have a different frequency and vibration so I can tell who I am receiving the message from. Ashtar always announces himself when he comes through and says, "This is Ashtar of the Galactic Federation of the Light," so it's pretty obvious when he comes in. I usually respond, "I know who you are," and start laughing when he starts with the formal announcement. Out of all of my guides, he is the most serious.

We often get information, hunches, nudges, or think we are hearing a voice, etc. but we write it off as crazy. We have no idea where it is coming from or why we should pay attention to it. This is where trust and faith start to come in. This is part of learning to open up and trust that you have your internal guidance system (GPS) and that it is just a matter of learning to follow it. Again, my spirit team thinks they are funny because as I am typing this, they are singing the Creed song "Higher" and then they go back to singing "Follow the Yellow Brick Road."

It is important to pay attention to these kinds of things as they are guidance. They are singing "Higher" because they are raising my vibration as I am writing this. They want me to be in better alignment with them so that the writing just flows and is in sync with me. They are singing "Follow the Yellow Brick Road" because they want me to trust that I am going to get to where I need to go with writing this and to get out of my head and just follow.

After my mother transitioned I was on my way to the cemetery after the service and I could still feel her close by. The ironic part was I said, "I will be talking to you more now that you are on the other side than I did before." That has turned out to be the truest thing. Every morning and evening of every day, no matter where I am, I see 8:23. That was my mom's birthday. So interesting that it started a few weeks after she transitioned. It is now seven years later and I still see it on most days and still find myself saying, "Hi Mom." She is the loved one who comes to visit and is around me more than any others. I find it very comforting now.

There was a time when I was sitting at my drawing table and both sets of grandparents and my parents were all standing on my balcony just sending me love and wanting to let me know they were close by. When I have situations like this now, I find it very comforting, but to be honest, it took a hot minute to get used to it. I did not handle it well at all in the beginning when they first started coming around. It started in dreams and then started to happen in my awake time. The progression for this gift was very slow and easy.

Everyone has two guardian angels that are with them all the time. The thing about angels is they cannot interfere with our free will unless we are in harm's way, and it is not our time to go. So, with that said, if you want help with something, ask your angels to help you. How many times have you prayed that something didn't happen? How many times have you lost something and asked for help to find it? How many times have you asked your angels for a romantic partner? Every angel needs a job, so ask. The more specific you can make it, the easier it is for your angels. Also, don't ask for something not to happen, instead ask for what you want to happen.

We all also have different guides that come in and out of our lives depending on what we are working on. One time when I was having a really hard time about two years ago, my spirit team sent a giraffe. I saw it for multiple days. I called him Geoffrey after the *Toys R Us* giraffe because it made me laugh and smile. The giraffe did not mind that I called him Geoffrey, I checked with him to make sure. The lesson I was learning at the time was to learn to see things from a higher perspective. When you are in the middle of the problem, like in the eye of the hurricane, it is calm. You cannot see the rest of the storm. Geoffrey said to try and look down at the situation and see if that changes your perspective and what you see. Sure enough, it did. Spirit wants me to also talk about having a bird's eye view, the same thing, just a different analogy. It is about having a change in perspective, and whatever analogy works for you is okay with them.

I am now going to share some channeled messages I have received from my guides. I am going to put the date the message came through and who it was from. While you are reading the messages, see if there is a change in what you feel, sense, or know. The energy can feel different while reading the messages.

A collective who died on 911 brought this message to humanity:

Don't ever forget. We all surrendered our lives on 911 as a collective to shift and change the world. What happened? There is more unrest, more hate, and more war. Remember how the world once came together after 911? Remember how everyone was a little kinder, a little more compassionate, a little more supportive? The world banded together. Where is that world now? Even with a pandemic raging in the world, Earth is at odds. Stuck in the old paradigm of fear, hate, and power. How does Humanity Shift? Does humanity want to shift? It is possible to shift if we all work together and band together again for the greater good. The old ways are disintegrating. One World, One Collective, One Humanity. One is all, and all is one. This is what the inhabitants of Earth need to remember. Today 9/11, 20 years later. This is a clarion call, a reminder. What choice do we want to make? What direction are we going to go? Can we all come together again?

September 2021

Healing Humanity

It is time to wake up and heal. You each carry a light and a spark, and when they are united in love, they light up the world. It is about connecting and seeing the similarities, not differences. For you are all human beings living on one Planet – Earth. You are all in this together, it is time to remember this principle, and what better time than Thanks-Giving? You are alive, breathing, and here to bring light, joy, and love. Once this lesson is learned as a collective, the human race/consciousness can move forward and evolve to where it is meant to be. Start to see the possibilities and choices, not the problems. This is our wish for you today and every day.

—The Galactic Council of Light 11.23.23

Sometimes as humans, you get stuck. Events, situations, and experiences happen to propel you in a different direction. It is all a matter of perception.

Start to see the big picture, not the individual situations. It is about a lifetime of soul growth, not one particular event, situation, or person.

Your life decisions all form the tapestry of who you are, and being human does not let you see the majesty of the tapestry.

Have trust, faith, and perseverance that all is unfolding as it is meant to.

Free will is about what event, situation, person, or experience is going to get you there.

A Collective 3.23.24

Dear One,

Today is Resurrection Day for me and about rebirth for you. Choose to make a declaration of what you each want for yourself and your life.

Resurrection is about celebration, rebirth, and Mercy. Take some time today and reflect on what this day means for you.

How do you show mercy to yourself and others? What do you need to let go of and not carry forward? What needs to be reborn in yourself?

These are just some interesting things to think about on this easter day.

Have faith in all that you are and are becoming.

Trust all will continue to be revealed and unfold as it is meant to.

Let go of needing to know the outcome, the hows, whys, and whats.

Learn to just fully be in the present moment, as that is all we have; the rest is an illusion.

Jesus 3.31.24

Questions to ask yourself:

How do you receive messages from your guides, angels, etc.?

Do you ask them for guidance and support?

Have you ever asked who your spirit team is?

Mantras and Deities

I have always had a fascination with Indian culture. In my freshman year of college, I wrote my term paper on the caste systems in India. The professor said no one had ever turned in a term paper on that before.

I have had some experiences with Indian deities in the past. For example, Vishnu and his bird Garuda were with me for years, to the point where other birds were almost sacrificing themselves on the windshield of my car or dive-bombing my head when I was outdoors. It was really interesting.

In 2022, I took a Mantra singing class. To say that the floodgates were open now would be an understatement. Every time we learned a mantra, I created a Mandala. I am going to share some of the messages that came up during this time.

I had an amazing teacher who was very compassionate and encouraging with me. As is normal operating procedure for me in classes, I had a different experience than everyone else. You never know what is going to trigger past life memories, experiences, or knowledge, and this class was no different for me. So much came up.

I am going to share some of the messages and experiences I had during my foray into mantras and yoga.

Radha Krishna Chant: Welcome home children. You are now connected to all dimensions through all time and space. The past and present are happening simultaneously. I was being shown all the deities having a party and dancing together, it was quite the vision.

Ganesha: Life is about joy; it is about being connected to what is truly important. All obstacles are removed when you are in oneness. You are connected and in the present. Trust and embrace the beauty that is all around. Breathe it in and commit to your path and your journey.

Buddha: The world and humanity need to remember that it is more than being in physical form. There are multiple dimensions and layers. Be conscious, be present, breathe. Breath is what is important. You have just forgotten. What is enlightenment? Enlightenment is about waking up from the dream and being in the present.

Hare Rama Chant: This one is meant to open your third eye to fully see with all senses and in all dimensions. It is about learning to see beyond the physical eyes. It is a high-vibration chant. Party song of its time. . . LOL.

Ocean Chant: Where the river and sea meet. Rise up to meet challenges, knowing you will have everything you need to be successful and be empowered. Learning to surf and ride the waves is an important lesson in life and humanity. Go with the flow!

Aham Prema Chant: I am divine love. Quan Yin came in and talked about compassion and love in all ways. Pink butterflies and dolphins were around.

Saraswati: Dear ones, thank you for connecting today. I love to share joy, wisdom, and peace and to help others. Learn to receive. She was singing with us today and facilitating an opportunity for each one of us to shift and transform, through sound, frequency, and vibration.

Not sure who was talking to me at this time: Dear One, you are being called home. You need to fully remember why you are here. They took me to the sacred temple in Tibet where some of these chants were conceived and put out into the world. I wanted to cry. It was so powerful and beautiful.

Gayatri Mantra: being the light. The best of humanity to uplift, heal, and inspire.

Sita Ram Mantra: Bringing us into oneness, wholeness, and finding our way. Spreading out the light and also balancing the light within.

Questions to ask yourself:

When you chant or listen to music, what comes up for you?

What do you do with the feelings, messages, or ideas you get when listening to music or chanting?

Is chanting going to be part of your spiritual practice?

Faeries, Butterflies & Dragonflies

One of my friends told me I should write a chapter on faeries. I have had many experiences with faeries who I experience as very mischievous and fun. I don't know how else to explain it; whenever they are around, I am always laughing.

I am now being shown the movie *The Blue Butterfly* where a boy has terminal cancer and his wish is to go to the Amazon to capture the blue butterfly. So many beautiful things in that movie, the aborigines and healing messages.

Butterflies have imaginal cells that are dormant until they go into the cocoon as a caterpillar. The imaginal cells activate while they are in the cocoon, and when they break out of the cocoon after their completed transformation into a butterfly, they fly. We as humans go through cocooning multiple times in our lives when we are in huge stages of change or when significant life events happen. Maybe it is time to think about all of these things and start to connect the dots.

So much has been left coded it is time to see the picture within the picture. We need humanity to rise above the 3rd dimension of duality to the 5th dimension of heart-centeredness. Animals are a big part of this transformation. Think about all the movies with animals. They are all captured at some point and at the end of the movie are released. . . What is that

telling humanity? We have all been captured or controlled for so long that now it is time for us to free ourselves and our consciousness. That is a big concept to understand, but from a higher dimension, this is what is wanted for Earth and humanity.

I have had many metaphysical experiences with dragonflies. I have also created many dragonfly mandalas. When I was little and went to the lake house my grandparents owned there were always dragonflies. I remember being mesmerized by them. It seemed like whenever I was on the pier or the water they were always around me. It never happened to anyone else in my family when they went outside. It was just so strange at the time. It makes sense now that I am older. I understand more about dragonflies now, what they represent, and the ancient knowledge and wisdom they carry.

Questions to ask yourself:

What do butterflies represent to you?

Do you talk to the faeries or elementals?

Do you feel connected to nature?

Dolphins, Whales and the Cosmos

In the movie *Avatar: The Way of Water* there is a scene at the beginning of the movie where the character is praying/chanting with beads. For me, this was a powerful reminder that what we see in movies is already happening. Immediately, I thought of praying with a rosary or chanting with a mala which is the meaning behind what is going on in the scene. There is so much for us to learn and such vast potential available for us human beings to tap into. There is so much about the oceans and space we do not fully understand yet. There are lots of messages if we are willing to pay attention and see them from a different, more expanded perspective.

I believe dolphins and whales are fifth-dimensional beings that came here to help guide humanity to the next levels of consciousness. When terrible things happen, you see whales and dolphins breaching themselves. I am being shown the movie *Arrival* which was about a cephalopod trying to communicate and give a message to humanity. There is much we need to learn and develop to live a peaceful coexistence on this planet instead of living in a way that is harmful to it and other beings.

Why do humans like swimming with the dolphins and want to go whale watching? There is something in our unconscious that lets us know they are here to help us, and we are trying to decipher what that is. We still have so much to learn about so many things. Our human brains are limited, but our soul or spirit brains can hold and retain so much more knowledge.

When I meditate, one of my favorite places to go is the Crystal City in the 5th dimension where there is pink water and pink and gold dolphins. I remember vividly the first time I was taken there in a meditation and had so much fun. I did not want to come back to the denseness of Earth and be back in a human suit. I could understand the dolphins.

They telepathically communicated with me, giving me information, messages, and mandalas to bring back for humanity. It was an amazing experience I will never forget.

I also have a very strong connection to the Mer people and have created many mandalas around them and their energy. I have always believed they exist, and have seen them many times in meditation and when I travel multi-dimensionally. There is so much that we as humans close ourselves off to. Now is the time to start remembering and be the most authentic version of you – you can be.

Questions to ask yourself:

Do you feel connected to the water, dolphins, whales, etc.?

Do you like to be in the water and feel like you are free?

Can you remember any past lives or experiences with the animals of the oceans?

Unicorns

Unicorns are making a big comeback right now as humanity's consciousness and awareness start to rise to a place where we can start to feel and experience this vibration again. Everything is always in divine perfect order and there are no coincidences. Everything unfolds exactly as it is meant to.

It is so funny to me how unicorns and sacred geometry are tied together. I never realized it until now. A few years ago I wrote a children's book called *Be Free to Be Yourself: The Magical Unicorn.* I didn't consciously understand the connection until now. The book was about a magical unicorn who used colors and symbols/mandalas to heal. . . it is just so funny how that connection never occurred to me until just now, years later.

This is how awakenings work. We get information or have experiences and our soul and spirit understand the importance of them at the time. But our consciousness files it all away until a time when we, as a human, are at a place where we can understand it and do something with the information.

To Humanity,

When it is the darkest it feels like all hope is lost and you don't know what direction to go. Remember, even during these times, there is still joy. There is still hope. There is still laughter and there is still love.

We, the unicorns, come at these times. Originally, humans thought we only came when energy was high, but now we come during difficult times as well to uplift, heal, and spread love and joy.

Some on the planet right now are the great healers and 7th-dimensional unicorns, and although there is no horn in this lifetime, healing is transmitted through the hands and heart.

The Unicorns 3.26.24

Questions to ask yourself:

When you think of unicorns, how do you feel?

As a kid did you ever play or talk to the unicorns or even now as an adult?

Can you feel the magic and pure hearts of the unicorns?

Section Three: Sharing What I Know

Teaching

For years, I have been told by many different people that I need to teach. For as long as I have been told that, I have been trying to figure out how to teach what I know. Teaching is still a work in progress for me. With that said, I realized that every time I do a reading, healing, or event, I am teaching. I am teaching how to be authentic, how to work past fear, and how to put our light out into the world.

I have always enjoyed less formal learning so I guess that is the kind of teacher I am going to be: less formal, fun, and sharing wisdom, laughs, and light. We have all experienced the truly weird, unexplained, and unexpected in our lives, now we just need to know what to do with these experiences. Someone always has to go first, and looking back on my life, that someone turns out to be me a lot of the time.

I have been asked multiple times how I share information with people when they do not appear to be open to it. My answer is that I ask questions. For example, if your loved one was here and said this, what would that mean to you? Do you see colors or flashing lights out of the corners of your eyes? Questions can sometimes be an easier way for people to receive the seed of knowledge or information and feel less threatened. Questions give the recipient a choice (free will), if you will, as to what they want to share, how much they want to share, and if they even want to answer.

There are so many different ways to phrase things and share things it is completely up to you as to how you want to do it. Trust your guidance, trust your instincts, and follow your hunches. It is funny, as I am typing this section of the book I am wondering when I moved from being the student to being the teacher. Don't get me wrong, I am still a student of so many things in life, and I am now also the teacher. It is a strange dichotomy at times. To be honest, the student role feels much more comfortable, and I know with certainty that this is also the time to push past that comfort and be the teacher that I am meant to be. Just as a point of reference, inside us, we all have everything we are. Sometimes we are the teacher, sometimes the student, sometimes the sage. . . We all have those parts to ourselves as we are all from the divine spark. It goes back to accepting, not challenging or judging. . .

We are meant to experience love, joy, and hopefully lots of laughter. How are you doing with that in your life? Joy and laughter raise our frequency and vibration and can bring about miraculous things in our lives.

One of the biggest things that comes up is that people ask me about the dreams and experiences they have in their Dreamtime. I have had many conversations with people who said my loved one came to me in a dream last night and it felt so real. I explain it is real, you are being visited and spending time with your loved one while you are in your dream time. The next question they always ask is why does it not happen in my awake time. The answer I have for this is oftentimes our loved ones do not wish to cause us any more discomfort. Sometimes if they come during our awake time, it is hard to say goodbye again, and brings up a lot of feelings for us. The more intuitive you become, the more all of the things that happen in your dream time will start to happen in your awake time.

One thing I try to instill in people I work with is that we all have gifts and abilities. As I said earlier, we sometimes get caught up in the way others do things and therefore feel like we are doing it incorrectly or something is not right. The biggest takeaway is to remember that however it comes, whatever it means to you is what is meant to be. Stop judging, stop analyzing, start accepting. This is the way forward. Trust me when I say this is still not easy for me. I love to question everything and think about every possible solution, and that is just a way to stay stuck. Just accept and move forward with what you know. Many times, we think what we have to say or share is not as important as what other people are sharing or saying. Spirit: YES, IT IS!

I have friends who do paranormal investigations, are transport mediums, intuitive, healers, etc. The bottom line is we are still in a human body and our physical brains have a hard time with some of this stuff. We can all do different things. We are all intuitive. We all get gut reactions to things. The trick is to start to pay attention to those reactions.

The other major problem with fully opening up to gifts can be past life experiences where you were killed for your gifts. For a lot of witches or people burned at the stake, having a sense of feeling unsafe has carried over. We will all be safe in this lifetime and that is part of what we need to remember as a humanity.

We all get different signs, for example, when something is true and important to share the whole left side of my head starts to tingle and vibrate. That is a sign for me that I need to pay attention. Other people see feathers on their paths, coins, license plates, and get feelings in their physical body. Start to pay attention to what happens to you as you get information. The more you pay attention, the more you develop your decoder ring and can move forward.

Questions to ask yourself:

What is my process?

How do you get information? Do you see, know, feel, sense, or a combination of all of these? Remember, there is no right way. Only your way.

What signs, songs, and license plates are you seeing, hearing, or feeling? There are messages everywhere all the time.

When you have a gut reaction, what do you do with it? Do you talk yourself out of following it?

Ancient Cultures and Knowledge

I have always remembered many things from past lives and ancient civilizations. In book One, *How I know what I know*, I was shown Egypt when my third eye reopened, how the pyramids were built, what they were used for, and where the capstones are buried. It is ironic, because when I was growing up, I wanted nothing more than to be an archeologist, but was so allergic to dust that was not going to happen. I did take an archelogy course in college and it was so fascinating to me.

One of the things I love to do is figure out solutions or missing pieces to things. My brain has always worked this way. I think this is pretty obvious from all the sacred geometry I use and the mandalas I create. I just assumed that everyone else saw the world the same way I did, but that was not a correct assumption. Some things are just so obvious to me it amazes me when other people can't see it.

Back to the re-opening of my third eye and seeing the history of the world and how we came to be. I have never been quite sure what to do with this information. I keep being told now is the time to share and teach it. There will be people reading this at some point who will relate. It is about putting it out there and taking the risk. What others think about it is none of my business.

Over the years I have created so many mandala codes and I always see them coming from the Amazon. There is so much knowledge and wisdom in this part of the world that we are still not fully tapping into. I am being told by my spirit team we all have an inner shaman, and it is about learning to listen and pay attention. Learn to follow your inherent wisdom and block out the noise of the world. Much has been left for us to figure out. So many human beings feel lost and disconnected. We all want to feel like we are a part of something. I believe this is why so many people want to work with indigenous people and learn the lost ways.

When I was drawing all the mandala codes of the ancient rainforests, I was guided to get crystal skulls. I was instructed to purchase 13 skulls and make a grid with them. There was something about re-opening the energy portal on Earth. Once I assembled the crystal skull grid I left it up for 24 hours and then was told to disassemble it. The portal that was needed was now open and protected. When you are awake, you are aware of so much more every day.

At this time on Earth, there is a grab for power, and different forces are still trying to control humanity and keep us from evolving. Just like in Atlantis, we are also at a point where we do not fully understand the technologies and energies we are using, which may create problems going forward. My Atlantean lifetime is one that still resonates the most with me in this lifetime. You can always tell who the humans are that had Atlantean lifetimes as they are the ones who love crystals. There is no such thing as too many crystals. . . LOL.

One of the things I never heard talked about is that all the pyramids of the planet are connected through ley lines into a system, just like the ley lines in the Earth connect into a grid. When they are fully operating, they provide energy and frequency to help light up the planet. You might say those were the first power girds of Earth. There is so much we still do not know and that we are still uncovering, and now is the time to start talking about all of it.

Questions to ask yourself:

Are there any ancient cultures or civilizations you feel drawn to?

If you travel, do you feel more connected to certain places than others?

DNA

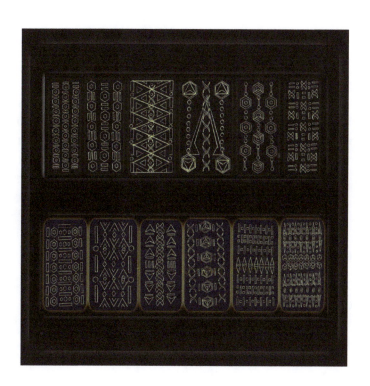

You have to love spirit and how it brings through messages. I was sitting in my living room relaxing and had just hung up with a friend after talking about how all day long I was getting ideas to write and then when I sat down at my computer everything went blank. I got up to wash my hands and I am not kidding you, the metaphysical jukebox turned on and my spirit team was singing "Start at the very beginning" from *The Sound of Music*. They are still singing as I am typing this. Does anyone else ever get messages like this?

I have been thinking about all the medical information I have gotten about DNA over the years and that is why they started singing "start at the very beginning." So here it goes. I talked about it in my first book, *I don't know how I know*. I was in an intuition class and after one of the meditations we completed, I started seeing DNA. It was everywhere, all around me. Not having had any science courses other than bio-1, I didn't know what it was, so I asked my instructor what are these grey tubes with purple balls on the end forming all these patterns with derivatives of 4 and 8? My instructor said it is DNA and to go back and quiet yourself to get more information.

So, I closed my eyes and saw all these patterns being created. It was really interesting. Like in the *Iron Man* movies, I could take my finger and spin it around. I was seeing it holographically, from all angles. I have never known what I was supposed to do with all of this information.

Over the years, I have drawn many healing mandalas. I have created 12-strand 3-tiered DNA mandalas. Recently, I drew what each strand of DNA looks like and then put the 12 strands together. This is the image at the beginning of this section.

One time I was at work, what I refer to as my day job, and one of my friends who does Neuropsychology testing was talking about a case. From her talking about it I could point to the part of the brain where the problem was. I just didn't know what that part of the brain was called. My friend was like, "OMG! I hadn't thought about that, but it makes so much sense based on what the testing reports showed." She thanked me. My friend said she knew what needed to be done now and how to help the individual. I was glad the information was helpful.

One of the things I have never talked about before is during Mr. Toad's Wild Ride week in the intuition class where all my gifts came back at once. I was told about genetic disorders, what causes some of them, and what kind of instruments need to be used to detect them. It was really interesting, but I still wondered what I was supposed to do with this information. I was told one day I would talk about it and meet the people I needed to meet who could develop what needed to be developed. I believe that the time is now.

I was also told 20 years ago that all healing will involve sound, frequency, and vibration, and work on healing the auric layers of the body and may not need surgeries or to cut into the physical body anymore. I feel like we are getting closer to that happening now. This information makes me think of all the *Star Trek* TV shows and movies where they just scan the body.

Back to DNA. As humanity ascends, our DNA ascends and changes as well. You often hear about ascension sickness, which is when our DNA is getting a reboot and throws off our whole field until it is rebalanced. I have to say that at times it is very strange to be so sensitive and see so much. At times, I could see, feel, and know my DNA was getting upgraded and my brain rewired. Sometimes I saw flashes of white light all around my head. I was never sure what to do with that information or who to share it with. My spirit team said it was important to talk about here because many other people have had similar experiences and they need to know it is okay, that they are not alone.

As I have said before, the language of the universe is symbols and our DNA is a symbol. The strands form patterns, and the patterns connect to make us whole. As I am writing this section right now there is a holographic model of DNA in front of me. My spirit team is pointing things out that, to be honest, I do not fully understand on a conscious level. One of the things I always thought was interesting was what I refer to as the purple balls on the end of the tubes that change colors based on the individual's health. Different illnesses have different colored balls on the end of the tubes. Genetic disorders are from tears in the tube part of the DNA. Some of the issues are genetic, and some of what we call genetic disorders are from environmental sources. There is so much we do not understand as humans about what effects are electromagnetic or in the biofield that surrounds us. We are not solid. Instead, we are thousands of moving pieces that look like they form a whole.

My spirit team is at it again, showing me the scene from the original *Willy Wonka* movie where Mike TV is sent into a thousand pieces and then reformed or like 'beaming up/down' in *Star Trek*. Depending on our thoughts, events, and situations, these pieces are put together to form us. It is so interesting when you stop to think about how magnificent the human suit is. Some of this is over my head, but I am just typing what I hear them say and letting them type some of it. This will make sense to some people who need to hear it.

Questions to ask yourself:

What kind of experiences have I had that I filed away because I couldn't explain them?

When hearing about DNA in this section, what feelings, thoughts, and/or reactions did you have?

Have you ever noticed flashes of light around you?

Me, Metatron, Sacred Geometry, and Mandalas

Ever since I took my first Opening to Intuition course 20+ years ago, I have seen and drawn mandalas. What I know about sacred geometry is that it is the language of the universe. Sacred geometry is symbols, vibration, frequency, love, and light. Sacred geometry is everywhere, in nature, in the foods we eat, and in the architecture of buildings. Sacred geometry works with our unconscious to bring information or knowledge into our consciousness.

Often people look at my mandalas and say, "They are so pretty, I love the colors or the pattern." The more you look at the mandala, the more they unlock. Archangel Metatron helps with distilling the knowledge and wisdom that is needed in each mandala. When you see pictures of Archangel Metatron, you will often see sacred geometry around his energy field. Archangel Metatron helps with spiritual understanding, learning, and knowledge.

As humanity continues to awaken, more people are becoming aware and seeing symbols, patterns, and the vibration of objects and not knowing what, how, and why it is happening. It is happening because the language of the universe is symbols and that is how information is being communicated. You may not understand it on a conscious level, but I assure you that your spirit and soul are getting the information they need and understand the transmission, as I like to call it.

When I was in that fateful class to learn about opening to intuition, we were going to make gift mandalas and I fought against it. I knew if I made one, my life would never be the same. I knew I would shift and shift quickly on some level. I have to admit, back then I was not as conscious of what was happening to me as I am now. All of a sudden, I understood things so differently. It was like someone turned a light on.

Every time I closed my eyes I saw mandalas and geometric patterns. I sketched them constantly. I stayed up all night in the beginning drawing these massive mandalas. Most of them had a medical flare to them, but I didn't know that at the time. It is interesting to look back to some of the mandalas I created in the beginning versus what they have evolved into now. The current mandalas are filled with so much energy and light that the planet was not ready for 20 years ago when I started creating them.

I have never had to study the principles of sacred geometry; they have always just made sense to me. I intuitively know what shapes to put together to create, etc. I always start with a blank piece of paper and do not measure anything. I just trust that the pattern that is meant to come through will. I am open to bringing forth whatever energy I am guided to bring forth and work with whichever benevolent being wants to come in to create it.

I am a pure conduit and most of the time I just get out of the way. I often listen to music while drawing to help with whatever frequency and vibration I need to bring forth. When I am done and I back away from the completed mandala, nine times out of ten I will say, "Wow! Where did that come from?" The tenth time is the mandalas I got to help cocreate and draw. I know the difference in the mandalas and the reactions from the mandalas.

The other interesting thing about the mandalas I create and bring forth is that no matter how many times they are reproduced, they still hold the original channeled energy and frequency in them. I have asked many times how that happens and have been told by my spirit team that it is not something I need to understand or concern myself with. I have learned to accept that as an answer although I find it difficult to do. I have always been what you would call a little stubborn and wanted to understand the things I was doing and how things worked. The gift for me is in letting go and trusting. Like other humans, I am still working on that one.

I find it so interesting to get feedback from others when they look and work with the mandalas. It is so fascinating to what gets unlocked for others and how they explain the mandalas and messages. I feel so blessed and honored to be able to create these energy portals (mandalas) for humanity to help us rise to where we need to be. I once received a phone call from a guy in the UK who asked me if it was normal for his room to dissolve around him as he looked at the mandala. I said anything is normal, it just depends on what we need and what gets unlocked. Nothing is really solid anyway. Everything is just vibrating so fast it appears solid.

One of my favorite things to do is to create custom mandalas for people that they need right now to help them move forward to wherever is next for them. The less information I know the more helpful the energy of the mandala will be, but sometimes people want to feel part of the process. Now I ask what their intention for the mandala is, and then I laugh because whatever they need is going to be brought to them through the mandala. It may not have anything to do with their intention but will have everything to do with what they need. . . I am not in control; I am just the conduit, and I get out of the way and allow spirit to create the masterpiece. Spirit even dictates the colors and brand of colored pencils I will be using to create the mandala.

I surrendered a long time ago, because if I picked what I thought the colors should be I usually ended up needing to create it in the colors that my spirit team wanted. I also find it fascinating if I listen to music and what the choice of music is, or if I am drawing in silence and what comes forth in either of those environments. Spirit usually dictates that as well. I have gotten much better over the years at paying attention to those details. Creating the mandalas is such a sacred process and I am so honored to be entrusted with this information.

Being human, though, we tend to doubt messages, symbols, coincidences, or synchronicities. We tend to downplay them because we cannot always make sense of what is happening around us. One thing Metatron wants to say is you must start to pay attention to all that is around you. Angels, Guides, Loved Ones, Ascended Masters, and Light Beings are always trying to communicate with us. The best way to describe opening your intuition and learning what symbols mean to you is to think about learning a foreign language. For some, it comes easily. For others, it takes a long time. Your intuition and understanding of what the sacred geometry/mandalas mean to you is based on what you need for your soul's growth.

I get asked how long it takes to create the mandalas and how many have been created. In the last 24 years I have probably created between four and five thousand mandalas. No two are the same, and depending on the size, complexity, and who is working with me determines the amount of time. Creating the mandala can take anywhere from 45 minutes to six hours. Some guides create faster than others. I always know when it is Metatron because I often hear myself saying I can't physically color that fast and he just laughs.

The mandalas have become my meditation practice and mostly how I channel. Wait, I am being corrected by Metatron. Metatron: that is the way you are the most comfortable channeling, not the only way you channel. Metatron is telling me like it is. I can voice channel if I choose to, but I prefer the mandalas and writing down the messages. Right before I started writing this section this is the voice/written message I received from Metatron.

Dear One,

Let go of fear and learn to trust. You know what you are doing, and you know I am working with you closely. Let it go and let it flow. Have faith as you are learning to do this, that all is being guided and will unfold as it is meant to. Focus on the experience and joy you are feeling as you are creating this and sharing it with the world. This is your passion, sharing, teaching, and being of service. This is who you are and have always been in this lifetime and many others. As you have chronologically aged as a human being in this lifetime you have grown into your gifts and abilities and your authentic self. Although you knew much of what you know now when you were younger, a certain wisdom and intention has come with age. This is the model you operate with for teaching what you know and have learned. Trust it.

Metatron

This is the time that humanity needs to wake up and shift. This is the time that humanity needs to understand that you are all light beings, souls, however, you want to think about it in a human suit. You all have gifts and potential that you are not even aware of. It is important to remember that thoughts are things, and what you think affects everything you do.

I, Metatron, will continue to work with the one writing this book to continue to explore the relationship between what is seen and unseen, what is felt, experienced, and how to use sacred geometry to unlock your consciousness to move and shift into the 5th dimension. It is time for humanity to ascend. That is what is happening on your planet right now. The battle of ascension versus that of being controlled. It is all tied together. It is all one tapestry. What do you want the tapestry to look like? How much of a conscious creator do you want to be with where humanity is going?

To say that Metatron and I have a strong connection would probably be an understatement. I did not realize it in the first two books in this series, but Metatron was guiding me as I wrote them and is taking a more active role in this book. Metatron keeps stressing the importance of teaching and getting all of this information out into the world.

I had a funny experience last night as I was working on my iMac computer and not my laptop. There were so many typos that Metatron said, and I kid you not, "I do not like typing on this keyboard, please go back to your laptop. I like the noise the keys make and the feel of the keys better." That seems like an easy thing to accommodate. So, this morning I am back on my laptop and Metatron is laughing as I am typing this. I have had many lifetimes where I have been connected with Metatron and understood and created sacred geometry. This lifetime is no different.

I find Metatron funny, kind, and often pushy. I don't know how many times I have heard I need to create a mandala on a certain day and answered I am tired and do not want to. LOL, the response I get is, you can do it now, or two in the morning, but it is coming through today.

Questions to ask yourself:

What guidance are you getting?

Are you allowing that guidance to come through?

Are you willing to follow the guidance you are receiving and trust?

Are you aware that everything in the universe has a pattern?

What do you notice when you look at certain shapes?

What kinds of reactions come up for you when you look at mandalas, portals, and fractals?

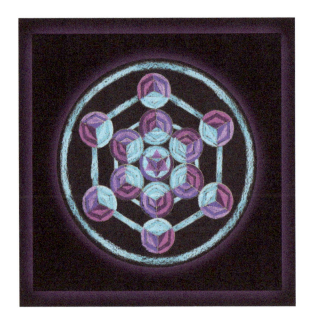

Epilogue

Thank you for taking this journey with me. I hope you laughed, questioned beliefs, and can see things from a different perspective.

To sum up: we are all a spark of divine light and currently, we are on planet Earth in a human suit. Being in a human suit causes us to forget we are light beings having a spiritual experience. Many of us wanted to come to Earth at this time for the shift that is occurring in human consciousness. We, the ones in the human suits now, are the lucky ones who got to make the journey.

Now is the time to remember who we are and break free from fear and control so we can transform.

Good Journey Fellow Travelers.

About the Author

Gail Alexander, No-Nonsense Intuitive, Life Coach, Author, Speaker, Medium, Therapist, and Multidimensional Artist

How often have you heard, "The truth is out there." Or "If you want answers, look within." And how many times was your response that you didn't have the first clue what to do with statements like that?

That's where Gail Alexander comes in. She actually does know. Gail knows how to access information for you that you haven't learned to find for yourself.

Gail has since studied many different healing traditions, including ARCH (Ancient Rainbow Conscious Healing), Angelic Healing Fire, DNA Theta Healing, EFT, Reiki, and Quantum Touch. Intuitively, she assesses which to use with each client and may draw on and interweave aspects of each. She is becoming especially well-known for the extraordinarily beautiful, energy-infused mandalas she channels.

One day we will all step into our ability to access the energy around us. Until then, whether it's physical, mental, emotional or spiritual healing, questions about those who have transitioned, or if something is out of balance in your life, Gail Alexander is honored to be of service to you and others looking for answers they feel are just out of their reach.

www.Gail-Alexander.com

Other Books by Gail Alexander

Mandalas Created for the World & Humanity

Energy Mandalas of Crystals & Stones

Healing Energies Mandala Coloring Book

I Don't Know How I Know. . . I Just Know

I Still Know What I Know

Jesus and the Jewish Girl

Bree Free to Be Yourself: The Magical Unicorn

The Great Awakening of 2020: A Mandalic Journey

Printed in the USA
CPSIA information can be obtained
at www.ICGtesting.com
CBHW062120250624
10635CB00033B/822